To

Chris

Jessie's Diary

Enjoy the
memory of
our 'Jessie'
with love
Lorraine

28/4/22.

Jessie's Diary

Published by The Conrad Press in the United Kingdom 2021

Tel: +44(0)1227 472 874
www.theconradpress.com
info@theconradpress.com

ISBN 978-1-911546-95-5

Typesetting and Cover Design by: Charlotte Mouncey, www.bookstyle.co.uk

The Conrad Press logo was designed by Maria Priestley.

Jessie's Diary

by Jessie Whitmore

Jessie Whitmore

June 30 1988 – September 6 2005

Note from the publisher, James Essinger.

I've decided to leave Jessie's diary with the spellings and punctuation that Jessie herself wrote. I think doing this best conveys Jessie's remarkable, resourceful and unforgettable personality.

Foreword by Lorraine Whitmore, Jessie's mum

My wonderful daughter Jessica did not imagine when she went into hospital for treatment for her leukaemia that she would never come out of hospital.

Her diary was supposed to just record her experiences; little did she know that one day her time in hospital would be shared by so many. She became wise beyond her years. If she could leave a legacy, it would be that family are so, so important. During her time her uncle, aunts, cousins all visited and took her out when possible. Everyone was ONE. She did not see what they could, a brave, strong, determined beautiful girl who was fighting to live, but had the odds stacked against her.

When she was taking her own last breaths before the machines took over, her aunt optimistically said 'Jessica, just rest and let the machine take over, it's like a tall wall to climb over, but you are strong'. I said, 'Jessica don't be afraid, nanny Barbara will look after you.'

Jessica left us in peace, thinking she had a strong family. Unfortunately her fragmented precious family are like strangers in the dark now.

For those who read this book, work hard to keep family together, money cannot buy the smiles and value a family can bring.

Lorraine Whitmore October 2021

The following article appeared in *Take a Break* magazine on January 5 2006 Issue 52/01

HOPE AND LOVE
JESSIE'S VOICE

Whatever else might befall Jessica Whitmore, her personality and character would remain eternal. Here her mother Lorraine, 48, explains

It was Sunday morning and, with the rest of the congregation, I rose to my feet and opened my hymn book. Just as I was about to launch into song I felt a disapproving glare shooting over me.

I was in church with my 12-year-old daughter Jessie and it wasn't the first time we'd been through this performance.

First came the furrowing of the brow, then the frown, then the stern shaking of the head.

She hissed: 'Don't do it, Mum, just don't.'

People around us were starting to look.

I raised one eyebrow and waited for her to deliver the final blow.

'Please don't sing, Mum. It's just too horrible.'

I frowned back at her.

Then we began to shake with suppressed giggles.

The thing was, I really was a terrible singer. But Jessie wasn't being serious.

In fact, nothing much was serious when we were together.

I'd wanted a daughter for as long as I could remember. My husband Geoff and I had an older son, Ryan, so Jessie was the baby of the family.

She seemed wiser than her years. She was always worrying about others – homeless people, frail pensioners, poorly children.

She'd say: 'Isn't it sad how people suffer?'

She always wanted to help everyone.

'Start thinking about yourself for once,' I said to her.

It made no difference.

When Jessie was 13 she said: 'I've met a gorgeous boy called Lenny. He's the one for me, Mum.'

I was pleased for her but they were still very young. However, as time passed, something became clear – Jessie and Lenny really were made for each other. They got on amazingly, despite some differences.

Jessie did well at school. She loved English and wanted to be a journalist when she grew up. Lenny on the other hand hadn't attended school regularly and Jessie worried that he was wasting his talents.

One day she sat him down at the kitchen table and laid her school books out in front of him. She went through them, painstakingly teaching him all that he'd missed out on.

'You'll go far if you make an effort,' she said.

She saw the potential for good in everyone.

Other times she was just like other teenagers – mad on handbags and shoes, and anything pink and girlie.

She made weekly trips to the shops and returned laden with bags.

Sometimes I'd go too, and we'd spend hours choosing outfits together.

One day she said: 'When I have babies I'll dress them in such trendy little clothes.'

She loved looking after Lenny's baby niece, saying to me: 'For a few hours I can pretend to be a mum.'

I'd always dreaded getting old but I found myself looking to the future and imagining Jessie grown up and bringing my grandchildren round to stay.

I knew she'd be a natural. She was a ball of energy, always charging around full of madcap ideas.

But just before she was 16 something changed.

She was constantly tired and her tummy became swollen. Then mysterious bruises appeared on her arms. Our GP referred her to hospital for tests.

When the consultant called us back, Lenny and I went with her. We waited in silence for the results.

Jessie had leukaemia.

As the doctor's words sank in, Jessie looked at me and burst into tears. She said: 'Mum, I'm scared.'

'Don't be,' I said. 'We're all here for you and we'll beat it together.'

But secretly I was terrified. Visions of the future dissolved and my head buzzed with questions.

Why this? Why now? Why Jessie?

This wasn't the way life was meant to be.

THE WORDS THAT LIVE ON

Now Jessie began making her notes. What would they reveal about her hopes and fears? Here her mother Lorraine continues her story.

We all just sat there, too shocked to say anything as the doctor spoke.

He said: 'Jessie, you must start taking medication. It may or may not work.'

'What if it doesn't?' she asked.

'You could have a bone marrow transplant.'

She forced a smile.

'Well, that's that then,' she said. 'That's what we'll do. This isn't going to spoil things for me. I'm going to carry on as normal.'

The doctor warned that the cancer treatment could leave Jessie infertile so she agreed to have some of her eggs frozen.

'I want to be a mum one day,' she said. 'This illness can't take that away from me.'

Her dad Geoff took her to the hospital every day for two weeks while the procedure was carried out.

After that she stayed true to her word, carrying on as normal despite the heavy medication she was taking.

She continuing to attend school and go off on her shopping adventures. She still looked tired but you'd never have thought she was so poorly.

If I tried to fuss over her she'd say: 'Don't treat me like an invalid.'

She went back to hospital for regular check-ups.

One afternoon I was sitting in the waiting-room with her when we got talking to one of the other patients. He said that he had to stay in hospital on his birthday.

Later Jessie said: 'I couldn't stop thinking about him all afternoon. Isn't it sad that he's so poorly on his birthday?'

I thought: *Typical Jessie*.

I said: 'Jessie, you're ill. You have to stop thinking about other people and concentrate on yourself.'

After six months something became clear – the medication wasn't working.

The doctor said: 'We need to find a suitable bone marrow donor.'

Months passed and it was proving difficult.

We had to do something so we launched an appeal in the local newspaper. We asked readers to volunteer to be tested and 100 people came forward.

One day the phone rang. Jessie answered and then turned to me, grinning.

'They've found one, Mum,' she said. 'They've got a donor. Everything's going to be all right.'

Her optimism was infectious and I started planning for the future again.

But first we had something special to celebrate – her 17th birthday.

We threw a big party and invited all our family, friends

and neighbours.

Jessie was right there in the thick of it all night, wearing a new brown dress she'd chosen specially and dancing away with her cousin Tara and best friend Daisy.

She looked gorgeous. In fact she seemed to glow. No one would ever have guessed she was ill.

But she was, and before we knew it the day we'd both been hoping for came.

Jessie went into hospital and the bone marrow was transfused into her body. Afterwards the doctors said they believed that it had been successful.

She was taken to an isolation ward to recover but was still allowed visitors.

The next day my sister Debbie arrived and handed her a parcel. Inside was a note pad.

'It's a diary,' Debbie said. 'You can record your thoughts in it while you are getting better.'

Jessie's eyes lit up. She turned to the first page and wrote: *Jessie's voice.*

Then she turned to the next page and began scribbling away. And as soon as she'd started there was no stopping her. When she'd finished, she looked up and said: 'You can read it if you like, Mum.'

When she was asleep I had a look:

Day one: After the transplant.

I feel weak and fat in my face and belly.

My mouth tastes like metal. I lost five hairs today… a sign I'll lose all my hair soon.

But I'll take one day at a time.

Her words were strong and brave but lying there she looked so vulnerable. Geoff and I took it in turns to sit with her.

The next day her brother Ryan came to visit. Jessie's hair was disappearing and she was very upset about it.

He gave her a hug and said: 'Sis, you're still the most beautiful girl in the world.'

And with that she grabbed her note pad and began scribbling away.

Day two: Good things about not having hair.

1) Don't have to wash, blow-dry or straighten it.

2) it's cheaper to maintain.

3) I get more sympathy.

4) It's cooler in the summer.

5) Won't get spots on horsehead.

6) It's neater.

7) No dandruff.

When she had finished she was grinning.

Later she wrote something else and then showed it to me.

'It's my plan for the future,' she said. 'Once I get out of this place I am sticking to my rules.'

Never smoke or be a passive smoker. Only drink on special occasions. Try to stick to a healthy diet and never go on a sunbed.

I was glad she was still looking ahead.

Jessie thrived on being around people and hated being on her own. We made sure there was always someone with her, even if she was asleep.

One night I had another look in Jessie's diary.

Day 10: this experience is making me realise just how much my family cares but Mum shines above everyone else. I realise how much she means to me and the way I love her so, so, so much.

I cried a little.

Although she was very weak, Jessie's doctor was pleased with her progress.

He said: 'You might even be able to go home soon.'

'Good,' she said. 'The minute I get out of here I'm going shopping.'

She started scribbling in her diary.

Day 11: Things I need to buy!

A nice big bag, some expensive boots, a big thick winter coat and gloves, jumpers, trousers, shoes, jewellery.

I read over her shoulder as she wrote her list and I said: 'I'll take you and you can have whatever you want.'

Some days we took Jessie out to the hospital garden.

Lenny would come too and we'd all sit there chatting about the future.

One day Jessie said: 'I'll take my A-levels and go to university. Then I'll become a journalist and start my life all over again.'

She turned to Lenny and said: 'You should make plans too. You should enrol at college and get some qualifications.'

She was still mothering everyone, even now.

Instead of complaining to us she wrote it all down in her diary.

Day 21: I don't think I can stand it here much longer. I hate it. All I do is sleep, poo, drink and throw up. Dad and Mum are brilliant though. I love them so much.

I cried a little again.

As time passed, something became clear.

I wasn't about to take Jessie on her shopping expedition any time soon.

The transplant had gone well but Jessie's organs were weakening. She was finding it hard to breathe.

The doctor told her: 'We may need to put you on a ventilator.'

Then he said something else and Jessie listened carefully.

Afterwards I couldn't get the doctor's words out of my head.

I'm afraid that if you go on a ventilator you probably won't wake up.'

Jessie was transferred to intensive care.

She was struggling to breathe and the doctor came to see her and said: 'We must put you on the ventilator now.'

Then a flash of something crossed her face.

Fear.

It was gone in an instant as she smiled and said: 'Don't worry. I love you all and I'll come back.'

She was still worrying about how we felt. She didn't want us to be upset. It was our feelings that concerned her most, not her own.

So Jessie was put on the ventilator.

She slipped into unconsciousness. We all sat with her

for a while – me, Geoff, Ryan and Lenny as well as other friends and relatives.

I kept thinking: *She's going to wake up any moment and give us a big grin.*

But she didn't, and after three hours she slipped away. She was 17.

We held her funeral near our home in Haven Close, Swanley, Kent.

The church was bursting with mourners.

After the vicar's address, we stood and prepared to sing a hymn.

The music started up and a butterfly appeared and darted between the mourners. It rested just in front of us. I could almost hear Jessie giggling beside me.

Jessie's been gone four months now. The house feels so empty without her but reading her diary is a comfort. When I do, she's back by my side and she's saying: '*Don't worry, Mum. I'm fine.*'

Her voice lives on.

Jessie's Diary

24/07/05

10.15 am: Start to write the diary of the start of my new life the start of my transplant.

Drove to Kings I had my bloods taken then I was examined by the doctor then went to Guys and signed in at Samaritans Ward.

"You are my sunshine, my only sunshine. You make me happy when I am sad."

SMOKING KILLS!

Mum's room No. 216

Then went for something to eat round the corner at a resteraunt/bar called Slugs & Lettuce. Free drinks – stupid bar man.

After dinner came bk to the ward with my mum. We had a chat and I wrote in my diary & saw the doctor & slept.

11.00 pm – take my bloods & flush my Hickman line.

12.00 am – they make me take 900mg of epletsy tablets! The doctors keep waking me up. I couldn't get to sleep.

'NURSE I'M HUNGRY, NURSE.

Monday 25/07/05

Mouth wash. Steroids & anti sickness.
Lenny   ❤   LEN

25/07/05

7.00am – the nurses woke me up for radiotheropy. I am so tired. 7.25am – they give me medication and took my blood pressure & temperature.

9.00am – Lenny came to the hospital and we have to sit and wait for peggaty.

Oh happy days!
When Jesus walked

Jessi's Voice

'U are my
Sunshine my
Only sunshine
You make me
Happy when I
Am sad.'

JESSICA

Written by Tara – voiced by Jessi

This was one of the most emotional days for young Jessi. She didn't get much sleep last night & was very frail and melancholic.

Tara (her cousin) had stayed the night. Lorraine (her mother hen) came at 6 am and showered the room with her lively presence.

Jessi was not very talkative and was very distressed and the only thing that calmed her down was Tara tiggling her back. Later Aunty Nikki, Lucy (cousin) and Laura (cousin) came to visit. It all got a bit too much for Jessi and she could not keep the tears in for much longer. Then the sickness came along with the tears and she collapsed in the toilet with her mum (the person who has been with her through thick and thin). Previous to this Jessi had the runs on her bed causing a bit of a mess.

As Jessi was crying a river in the toilet the tearfulness spread to Tara who said that she "had to let it all out". Then it spread across the room. We finally left Jessi to get some sleep and she felt better after. On return her bay

Written by Tara – voiced by Jessi:

Jessi has been violently sick three times this morning and all she can taste is self-conceived metal that is being over her mouth. As Jessi sits strenuously trying to do her puzzle, she feels bloated and as though she's going to pop.

Jessi is repelled by the two Nurse Helen's. She only wants to be helped by Nurse Laura. But unfortunately Nurse Laura can not be reunited with Jessi until she returns from her trip to Africa, where she plays with elephants.

5/8/05

Yesterday my baby had her transplant (37yr male) every male that came in the room we asked if they were 37 yr we owe Jessie's life to this kind wonderful man. Very drowsy throughout the transplant. Mum and Dad went to the café in the meantime – Ryan visited at 11pm but Jessie was very tired. Didn't sleep too well slept 1hr in my bed 2hrs in Mums bed then slept in chair for a short while. Jessie never complains and accepts all the different side effects that happen so brave. I love her so much. Mum xx

Lenny visited 2day and brought me a new CD. I cried and was sick. I hate this place. I wanna go home.

I feel weak and fat. In my face and belly. I hate the taste in my mouth – it tastes like metal. I can feel ulcers coming on my gums. I want to eat but when I try even my favourite tastes, are tasteless.

My hair feels itchy – real itchy. I lost 5 hairs today, the nurse said the itchiness is a sign that I will be loosing my hair soon. The Haematologist Consultant said 'everyone' worries about loss of hair at this stage, but by the time I start to loose it in 'clumps' I will be feeling sooo aweful it will be the last thing on my mind!

Eyes feel heavy, tired & blood shot. Hospital is not a good place if you want to sleep. Constant, visitors, nurses, norses. I feel I only want my family now and my boyfriend lenny. As nice as my friends are I would rather see my family as I can't and don't want to make the effort to talk. However there is a few friends I'm happy to see.

My face feels chubby and bloated with spots, fortunately the spots don't show too much as the radiotherapy has tamed my skin.

Tonight my Aunty Deby stayed the night. I fell asleep while she did 'Spider man tickling on my back. Before I slept I told her that I cannot see the end of this aweful feeling and do not know if I will be able to get through it.

More IV treatment for 2 hrs then I may get an uninter-rupted sleeps, oopps more pills, more nausea. It will all end, I will take one day at a time.

Betty is in her nighty tonight. She had her purple bumble fee outfit last week. BEE there for me betty!

"I said to the doctor I want to go home cause I felt so bad today and the doctor said to me

"Well you can't make an omelette unless you crack a few eggs"

which he meant you can go home but you wont feel better.

Day + 2

05-08-05

I had a good night sleep last night best yet. My Aunt Debs stayed with me and let me sleep in her bed.

Today I feel more positive and am thinking much clearer about the next few weeks. Just a couple of doses of aunt Deby and everything sounds better.

good things about Hair

- Look prettier
- different styles

- keeps you warm
- Protects your head
- fringe covers your spots
- play with your hair
- sign of youth

bad things about not having hair
- don't have to wash it, blowdry or straighten it
- cheaper to maintain
- get more sympathy
- cooler in the summer
- Hair grows bk better
- you won't get spots on forehead
- neater
- no dandruff/Grease

Today Aunt Nikki cut my hair really short however there was no need as my hair started to fall out my pubic hair as well.

My pledge for my new future.

- NEVER SMOKE, OR BE A PASSIVE SMOKER
- ONLY DRINK ON SPECIAL OCCASSIONS!
- TRY TO STICK TO A HEALTHY DIET.
- Never go on a sunbed!

TANYA & CAROLINE CAME TO VISIT.

Starting to realise Lenny actually doesn't care and today he really pissed me off!!!

Day + 4

7th August 05

Jessi feels a lot happier and positive today. Mother hen & goose went to a wine bar to drown their sorrows. Lenny & Tara stayed with jess and me watched Hitch. Jess showed every one her party trick, where she pulls out a clump of her hair.

Tara was horrible to me today as she made me drink! How horrible she is!

Tara is being so good and supportive and I appreciate her so much just like my aunt Debs.

Tara gave me a really lovely card today it meant so much to me and really does prove how much she cares.

7th August

DAISY WOZ ERE LOVIN JESSI!

DAISY BEAR TO JESS!

What an adorable bear!

Jessi shaved her hair off today because it was itching her. She did No. 8 then went down to a No. 2. She was so brave, but it doesn't matter because she still looks a rite old stunner, such a natural buet!

Aunt Niki stayed with me last night. She is so kind and her and uncle Billy have been Brilliant!

Day + 5

8-8-05

Today is my nan's birthday they came to see me but I slept most of the time because I was a bit knocked out on some of the medication I had in the morning! Also today I had my cocaine mouthwash and morphine for my throat, for the first time. My cousin Ty came up to see me today he was so nice to me. Saraya really annoys me the way she's acting towards him. Mum went and met Phil for a drink, mum likes phil she makes her laugh I'm glad gives her time to herself and not worry about me so much.

Mum got 1 big wart had to put some stuff on it for her.

My nurse (Emily) today is so nice I glad she's back tomorrow, when I've got a nice nurse the days don't seem as long or as bad.

Ryan my Bro came to see me today (2nite). This time in hospital has made me realise how important my family is and caring they all are. This awful time brings the best out in people, like my brother although he doesn't really no what to say to me everything he does proves how much he cares & loves me.

Had a good night sleep but I did have some cocaine mouthwash and morphine at 3.00am but I slept through 'till 6.30am when my dad brought in my mum a cup of tea. Muma stayed again.

Its my nurse Emily's birthday today. 26th bday. Both Laura and Emily are in today which means Im going to have one of my good days today. Had to have an x-ray done this morning, I had to sit there for about 1½ hours and while I was down there I saw so many ill people most with cancer this disease takes so many lives its arwful.

Caroline came to see me & brought me some DVD's in.

11.55am: Had some more cocaine & morphine. My aunt Niki, Clare, Lucy came to see me and me Nikki and Caroline finished the 3rd puzzel.

4.00pm. Had some more morphine & mouthwash

Romina and Linda came up to visit me there both so lovely, they brought me a big card & balloon up. Hopefully I will see them again soon.

Mum went to see Phil today and my dad stayed with me until 6.00 when I had my next dose of morphine & mouthwash.

WATCH BRIDGET JONES DIARY!

LENNY got on the wrong train to Elephant & Castle so he took ages to get here.

Starting to think I've been really nasty len, he does care he just like a normal man/boy and really doesn't no what to do or say in this situation! I no it's hard for him to but sometimes I just take the horrible time out on him.

Lenny brought Dave Rogers up the hospital today and left him from 6.30 8.30 downstairs in the cantine!

He also brought me some new white converse trainers.

CONVERSE

9.15pm – Had morphine and a bigger dose of cocaine.

Got Nurse Olivia on tonight and Hawkings who takes my obs – I like them both there really nice.

Me and mum watched roots once again but she fell asleep half way through. In tonight episode of root Kounta Kantay had one of his feet chopped off

❤

Day + 7

Last night wasn't to bad but I had a drip on all night and my throat is so sore. 3.00am – medication – morphine & mouthwash.

7.35am – next dose of morphine & cocaine.

Mum lefted about 10ish as Brian brought Tara up as she is staying with me all day.

We watched a film called Raise your Voice!

11.17am – had more morphine & cocaine

Got Nurse Kate today she's nice. Had my top stitches taken out today.

Temperature went up to 38°c.

Jessie is finally drinking – she likes Mars Drink. She's had a lot of cocaine today. – She craves cocaine. She wishes that she could swallow it so it would numb her throat. (And so she can get high).

Tara is not good entertainment as she's a sleepy bunny. Geoff came to visit.

Watched 6 episodes of Gimmie gimmie! Tara had a sleep while me & my dad watched them

6.00pm – had more morphine & mouthwash.

Letter from my Donor!

It means so much to me this man must be very special.

Me, Tara and Aunt wrote a letter to the donor from me.

Aunt Debs is staying with me.

What can I say: My Jess, my baby I have come from work – starving, caught in horrendous traffic, only here an hour. Jes let me go out & meet my mate Phil for something to eat.

On return, she tried to make my evening stay pleasant & watch a DVD, I knew she was completely knackered.

BP 122/78. Temp 37.6. I asked nurse to give her some nutritional drinks. Jess tried but said it was 'orrid' I can hear her coughing in the loo.

hope she sleeps tonight.

Me and Debs watched pretty women – my favourite film.

Last night I felt sick and really wanted to throw up but couldn't as there is nothing in me to be sick.

Day + 8

11-08-05

Had another good night sleep last night and I am now having a bigger dose of morphine & cocaine mouthwash every 4 hours the mouthwash works really well.

Got Nurse emily today. She's gonna give me my 3rd dose of methatrate (chemo). I really like emily she so good at her job & really friendly.

Just had my 3rd lot of methatriate and saw the pain. Specialist made my dose of morphine bigger as my throat is so sore, still on cocaine mouthwash as well.

Try to shave the rest of my hair off with a razor but didn't really work just got a little bit more of hair to go and I will be one bald bitch!

Had a cup of soup today – I'm very proud of myself.

Doctors came to see me today and said that I'm doing really well.

Dad came up about 4.30 today – I love my dad so much!

Emily is not back on till Monday and I bet I have crap nurse all weekend!

Kelly & Brooke rang nice to hear from them both coming to see me next Sunday.

Had my first injection in my stomach tonight this injection is to boost my white cells I will have this injection everyday until I am well enough to come home.

Drank enough liquid today so I don't have to go on a drip tonight.

My bro & Daisy came up tonight. I felt sick again tonight but still couldn't bring anything up, it really hurts my throat!

Twinle twinle little star

"Diamonds are a girls best friend!"

Day + 9!

12/8/05

Had a good night sleep last night. Had some morphine & cocaine at 2.30am!

Hawkings & this nurse was on last night they were both nice.

Woke up at 6.15am dad brought me & mum a cup of tea in and I drank all mine

The last root DVD is broke!

My Uncle Billy & Cuz Clare come up nice to see them they have all been really good and I appreiate them so much, for all the things they have done for me & the way my whole family has been so caring and supportive.

Lenny got has tattoo done today they started around 12ish and finished at 3ish.

My nan & Gramps came to visit. I done my nans nails.

Jessi swallowed cocaine (by accident).

Jessi's highlight of the day was when Tara & Ty came to visit.

Her downside was when she woke up coz her throat was hurting, and she thought she looked like a proper cancer victim.

Tara stayed till 10.30pm last night the dirty stopout as we watched big brother to see Anthony win!

Really like Tara's dress – she looked really good in it!

Lenny came to visit tonight my poor baby is in so much pain from getting his tattoo done. It looks really good on his bk best tattoo Ive seen!

Ty came to visit also tonight aswel but only stay 30-45mins cause he had to meet 1 of his friends.

Lenny didn't stay long as he was in too much pain so he only stay about hour/hour an half.

Tatoo looks sexy aswel! V. Manly.

My lenny tattoo but it doesn't look like that so it's not Len tattoo but he had 1 like that done but 10 times better.

Day + 10

Had another good sleep last night must be betting use to the bed!

Woke up a 6.30am this morning half an hour later that usually! Then had my drugs!

Already had 4 drips this morning and my bloods taken.

Dad brought me & mum tea up.

Today is gonna be another one of my good days today as my nurse is Laura!

Laura so nice she's like a mate aswell as a nurse cause she just comes in my room for a chat sometimes but what makes the best of it she's good at her job.

Bill, Nikki, Laura & Lucy have gone to Dubi today. Lenny here today got here bout 11.30ish and is staying with me all day. He looks a bit wored out and tired.

He looks pretty in Pink today.

Dad came bk to my apartment today 12pm left a 2.05pm.

Laura gave me & Lenny a playstation and some games for us to play but Len was the only 1 that played he was glued to the game as usual, he was even shouting at the game!

Lenny was really good today, he got worried about Daisy's smokers cough but I will be fine! He left at 6pm! I Love lenny

36

Daisy got to my gaf about 3pm today the 5mins later Christina got her. They both stayed with me until 9ish we watch cruel Intentions and talked about old times when we all young and use to hang round the streets together! (What tramp!)

Daisy brought me some presents today she got me a dream catcher, special friend guardian angel, a braclet & necklace that is meant to keep you healthy and a best friend card! They were all very nice and I beleive in all the things she brought me. And crazy daisy blessed my room for me with her magical powers!

Dream catcher brought by daisy to stop stop stop my nightmares

I   daisy

❤   &

Len   jess best mates

❤

Jess

Got an agency nurse on tonight she's crap but no need to worry as patience is here aswel & checks up on me – I like patience.

SMOKING KILLS!　　SMOKING CAUSES CANCER

<u>NOTE</u> FOR next person that reads the diary, IF YOU ARE A SMOKER STOP QUIT AND CONTINUE TO READ! OK!

Write ur name on this Page if you want but find it hard to quit as I will give you my powers to stop!

Smoking seriously harms You and other around you!

Day + 11

14/8/05

Last night I had a brilliant sleep & I didn't get up until 8.30am. Laura is my nurse today. She is bk on Tuesday doing nights.

Lenny got to the hospital bout 11.30-12pm

THINGS I NEED TO BUY!

Bluewater here I come!!!

- A nice big expensive bag either from Russel & Bromley or house of frazer.

- Nice pair of expensive boots also from Russel and Bromley.

- 2 pairs of timberland boots – 1 of them the trainer ones from choice

- bobble hat, scarf and gloves.

- A big thick winter coat

- Jumpers, trousers, shoes, jewllerey.

Aunt debs came to visit me today and jack sat outside in his car, think he got annoyed my mum went out with Phil!

Took picture of Laura, Ellen & I as they wouldn't take 1 yesterday.

My whole body is dry and sore as the radiation has burnt parts of my body my hands & feet especially.

Lenny left about 3.00pm and me and my mum were left on are own.

then Amy & Daisy came to see me & daisy was so funny and it was nice to see amy, I liked her trainers. Wish I could see madds.

They both didn't leave till about 11pm! Thier coming to see me tomorrow as well.

Had Laura today, that why we had a good day today. She bk on Tues/Wed doing nights!

15-8-05

Had an agency nurse last night but he was ok that makes a change.

Woke up this morning and my throat & mouth was really sore. I got up at 5.30am and had my morphine and cocaine then!

felt really weak and tied today I need to catch up on my sleep and start doing some exercising.

Got nurse Emily today I like having her, Emily & Laura are my best nurses.

Emily gave me my last dose of chemo today, most people only have 2 doses of this Last chemo but I've had the whole 4 doses! Now during the next week my mouth & throat are suppose to get worse, I will wait and see first though.

Lenny was suppose to be here at 11.00am and it 2.00pm and he's still not here. THE PRICK! Lenny arrived at my apartment at 4.45pm!

6ish I can already feel my mouth & throat getting worse.

Me and Lenny had a nice night just the 2 of us. We both stayed up until about 1am and watched the film second hand Lions.

Although I was on drips all night and my mouth & throat were really sore I still had some sleep.

Day + 13

Got up at 5.30am cause of all the drips I was on all night.

Lenny left at 10am because he had his interview at Bromley college, if he gets in he starts in September, Len said it went well.

Was on my own until 2.30pm when my aunty Debs. Nan & Gramps and dad all arrived I could hardly keep my eyes open. I was so tied.

Mum got back to the hospital at 4pm and I hadn't seen her since 11am yesterday morning I miss mummy when she doesn't stay with me. My lovely mum brought me a really nice new bag for me, Ruby & Millie make up brush & glass nail file. – Total cost £70.00 – Love all my new things but Love my mum more

Tara & Daisy came round we took lots of photos. Tara left about 9.30 pm and daisy left about 10ish.
Mother hen stayed with me...

Day + 14

Laura started nights last night, so I had my Nurse/mate looking after me didn't really need much though but she came in for a good old chimwagging.

Woke up this morning really tied, weak & stressed.

Was sick twice today and it has made my throat and mouth even worse. I had nurse Ellen on today She's really nice but she went on a meeting at 12.00 & then her lunch break and while she was doing those things I was sick 1st time about 12ish and I asked the helper to tell one of the nurses to get my morphine mouthwash but she forgot and I waited & waited then fell asleep and I was due a dose at 2pm which 1 nurse finally arrive with at 3.45pm!

That's when the godfather, Alan arrive and I was in such a bad, stress mood and I was so anger by the helper I was quite rude and was taking things out on my mum & dad! SORRY! But I then said sorry to everyone and explained what happen and all the pain I was in. I even cried I was so angry and pissed off!!

I then stayed called and relaxed for the rest of the evening.

I also had a little nap which helped.

But readers you wouldn't believe what the same stupid helper done again, this is how it all began…

I sitting on my bed about half 7pm and I was taking all my medication and when I took the last liquid which is meant to help me poo I threw up for the second time and this was worse, so I pressed the buzzer the help arrived so I parcificly said to her "tell Ellen I need my painkillers, I've been sick my mouths worse!"

It then got to 830pm I pressed the buzzer again and thankfully Ellen and Laura arrived to my room and I said to Ellen I need my painkillers and I asked if the helper told her she said no one had said anything to her that I was sick and really needed my painkillers.

HELPER – NEVER AGAIN – SELFISH WOMAN.

Laura began her shift she popsed in and out my place with drugs and for chats – good old Laura.

Ryan came up nice to see me old bro – he met Laura.

Me & my mummy watch DIB jepreody good film.

Day + 15

Woke up this morning and I've got a bloody temperature 37.9° and Laura had to put me on the oxygen machine.

Doctor the came in and examined me and couldn't really see anything wrong with me but put me on new antibioctics.

Got nurse Ellen today again but I don't mind as she nice and a good nurse

Had a really bad, long nose bleed with blood clots it was totally gross like ewwee.

All the doctors came to see me (Dr Sky).

Dad couldn't see me today because he was so filthy.
  Lenny stayed with me till 6pm & debs got her at Debs is staying with me tonight – we will have a good old chat

Laura is my nurse tonight! She Great

Started off my beautiful artwork today!

19/7/05

JESSICA'S MEDICAL REPORT

Aunty Deb here. Stayed the night Jes has x1 blood transfusion in the night. Jes tried peeing x 3 times over night. She gets a tingle feeling but cannot pass any water. We had intermittent snoring sleeps at 14.00 we spoke about 'Len' & his life. I hope so much that he makes the most of doing his carpentry course. (If he gets a place in September)

Jess had a temp of 37.9°c in the am she sounds snotty, her O^2 was low so is on oxygen. Dr saw her & said that although she cannot pee, she does not have a distended tummy. Lungs are clear. Dr is going to give 'Frusemide' tablet to make her pee.

Had a long chat this am with 'HAWKINS' the care assistant he used to do Psychy nursing but got attacked twice. I told him one in four Psychy nurses end up needing Psyhy treatment. I think Lorraine & I are potential clients we do strange things.

Not enough pictures for collage we want some 'recovery' pictures Jes spent 3hrs painting a picture for her mum. She wants to do one for 'Laura' the nurse as well.

geof the 'dear' bought in tea & toast at 6 am. Lorraine rang to say at 4 am Ryan smashed a flask of coffee all over kitchen. Bet Geof not a happy bunny. Poor lorraine had to clear the mess. While her hair was yelling out 'I want to be washed!

Day + 16

Woke up this morning bout 6am then daddy dearest brough me & Debs a cup of tea and some slices of toast for deby.

When I woke up in the morning I remembered that I was sleep talking because I kept dreaming things and talking back to one things in my dreams.

My oxygen levels are low again so Ive got the pipes up my nose again.

Debs left 11.30pm and dad arrived about 12pm and we watched the dukes of Hazzard

Then I went for a heart echo and tummy scan to check all the things were working.

Mum came up when I was having my scan my spleen & liver have enlarged. No total danger though.

Slept for the rest of the day I couldn't keep my eyes open woke up about 9.30pm.

Ryan pop in today to give me some presents he brought for me, burt and betty.

Day + 20

23-8-05

Haven't wrote in my diary for a few days as Ive been so worried out all the treatment I have had has drained everything out of me. I have felt so weak and couldn't be bothered to do anything but sleep.

Day +18

21.08.05

Last night Daisy stayed with be and we watched the film as good as it get, it was ok but I was just really tired. Didn't have a very good night sleep because I was on drips all night, and the nurses were in & out all night long. Mum got to the hosiptal about 2am because she was worried about me and had to sleep in the bed with daisy.

Today I had an x-ray dais came with then I slept the rest of the day until 4pm when me, Laura and mum when for a walk up Demark Hill Park it was nice to get some fresh air.

When I came back I had a nice sleep and woke up at 7pm – Then I was sitting on my bed and I had a urge to poo. So I went to the toilet and done lots of poo then I got cramp in my stomach & was really sick. Then I went bk to bed and had to have my last drips for the night.

Deby and Tara came visit me I slept and bit why they was here but got up for a good old chat.

23.08.05

Lenny stayed with Jessica. She is feeling sick and has a temp.
I came at 12.30 lenny left. Jes & I went to the Park and sat
on the grass we had a 'cafe laté' & jes managed a small bit
of a banana. Jes was obviously unwell as she wanted to go
after 10 mins. She had to sit down a few times. I got a wheel
chair for her & we went back to ward. Jes lay on bed while
I 'spider manned' her back. Sleep tight baby. Tomorrow I
am away in France till 11th Sept. I will miss you so much.
But, nice for me to come back and you will be, look & feel
so much better.

Love you babee jes
Aunty Debs

24/8/08

Still in hospital meant to be going home this week looks
like I've got a lot in this place I don't think I can stand it
her much longer I hate it here. All I do is sleep, poo, drink
and throw up.

I love my mum so much.

My nan and Grandad came to visit today nice to see them

Went to the cafe with my mum then went bk and sat with my nan & Grandad why my dad took her to the other cafe to have something to eat. My dad & mum are brilliant I love them so much.

Had some mouthfalls off Shepreds pie.

24-08-05

Jessi has just been told that she hasn't got a fungal infection. She is ☺ at this news. She feels she will be home soon. Also Laura the nurse is on duty tonight so she's even more happy. This is a room full of happiness.

Questions to ask Dr Sky:

1. How long till I get home?

2. What are the results from CT Scan?

3. When will the results come back to see if I have any bugs?

4. Do I need any more treatment?

5. Can I go home for the weekend?

WE HAVE A POO CONNECTION.

Jessi is making me feel guilty for going to Greece, even though I don't really wanna go.

Jessi feels she wants to get in a car and just drive for miles.

Still not home thought I would be home by now can't stand this place much longer but today I woke up with a much positive attitude to what is about to happen over the next week.

Mum here with me again she doesn't leave my side. I love her her being with me.

Debs has lefted me and she's not back until the 11th Sept and Tara is going to Greece on Sunday so they are both leaving me for 2 weeks.

Dr Sky and the rest of the doctors came to see me today looks like im in hospital for another week yet before I go home. God please let me be home by Tuesday/Weds.

Lenny came today about 2.00pm and left about 7.30pm it was nice to see him today I realise I have missed in and do need him cant wait until Im home and things start to become back to normal. 6-8 months.

Dad stayed with me today until 5ish and had to go because his metre ran out.

Mum went to see Phil for an hour when mum got bk Lenny left to see if he could get home in time for boxing training.

I can see my mum needs a break another week for me is as long as it is for me a week a month it sounds like to me & mum everyone else can come and go as the please but my mum stays by my side 24-7.

Day + 23

Friday 26th August

Today mum went to work and left the hospital at 7.45am and my dad got to the hospital at 8.45am but still brought in tea at 6am as well.

Aunt Nikki & Lucy came up today nice to see them both hopefully I get out of hospital on Monday for the day to go round Bill & Nik's for roast.

Done lots of walking today feel much stronger on my legs!

Patience said she cant see why I cant go home on Monday for the day.

Romina came to visit me today and cancelled her lesson for me. Really really nice to see her.

Lenny came to visit and stayed about an hour an half and got the train home with mina I cried when they left I wanted to go back with them.

Mum got bk before they left she had an argument with nan today.

I

❤

Mummy!

I WANT TO GO HOME!

Day + 24

27/8/05

Day by day its getting longer in this place im feeling so depressed I need to go home and start making a recovery there I can't think straight here I want my own surroundings this is really hard this week I feel Im gonna have a break down in here I cant cope much longer.

me & Laura went for a walk up the park today and had a good old chat and my Aunt Caroline came to see me today and my mum & her went to the cafe for Lunch. Got bk from the park and dad was in my room waiting for me.

woke up really down this morning but my chats with Laura really clear things up if Laura wasn't a nurse here at kings my time would be so arwful Laura has made my time here better and made me realise that I am here because I need to be and when I'm ready I will be able to go but if I leave now I'll be back within days for another month. LAURA MAKES ME REALISE ALL THIS – she's been great!

Laura on again tomorrow but got a week off hopefully

I won't be here when she gets bk but she's only a phone call away.

Dad is staying with me until Lenny gets here cause he is staying with me tonight because mum is going out with Laura!

I like being with my dad he is good to me!

Lenny got in a fight Last night now he mite be in trouble with the police – find out the whole story when Len gets to the hospital.

me and Len had a little cuddle cant want for a proper one. We watched x-factor, casualty and then a film on channel 4 Len stayed up to watch it but I fell asleep.

I LOVE Lenny!

Day + 25

Sunday 28th August

Lanny & I got up about 6ish then my mum came she was knackered when she got here. Mum then walked down to the cafe to get me a nice hot cup of tea.

When mama came back from the cafe with my tea Len left because he wanted a shower & that but he had to get a train to Bromley South and got a bus home from there he told me he got well pissed off! So would have I!

Len left about 8isham it 12pm am I miss him so much I want him here now I love my Lenny lots. I want a big cuddle & kiss!

Then about 12.30 my dad came and got me & mum and we walked down to Johnnies cafe and I had a roast dinner. Then my brother came and met us with 2 of his friends we walked up to the park & sat there for half an hour and had a drink & my Bro & 1 of his mates came up to my room for a while. It was so nice to see Ryan. I like his new tatoo.

3.00pm – Got 3 drips on! I've missed Ryan!

Got Nurs4e Laura Today but she's leaving at 4 and isnt in all week hopefully my last week.

I saw the doctor today – told me I've got a bone marrow test on Weds but the worst thing is my mum is not going to be there with me because she is going to work and Im not not going to see her until Thurs morning because Nikkis staying with me but that's okay I like Nikki staying.

Day + 26
Bank holiday Monday 29th August.

Going round Bill & Niki's for the day but it nearly didn't happen. My temperature was 37.5°c and the doctor came to see me before I left and was worried about my lip and wanted to give me platelets and would have to wait 2 hours for them & Billy was already waiting outside for me but the doctor said if my temperature had gone down I could go. I went "quick mum cold drink" temperature was 36.6°c! I can go. Met Bill outside the hospital he picked mum & I up in the Range Rover got bk to Bill & Nic's about 1.00pm everyone was there Lucy, Laura, Clare and dean. Had a really nice roast dinner ate as much as I could Laura Barabra's boyfriend was there to. After dinner we all sat outside and I drove Uncle Billy's tractor round the garden – that was fun! It was really nice weather today. Lucy and I went for a drive. Nikki done mum's hair She looks beautiful, Nik done mums hair really good & put some colour on her checks!

Left Bill & Nic's at 5.00pm after a lovely cup of tea cried because I didn't want to come back to the hospital. Emily the nurse brought me my platelets and another drip for my lip. Nurse Emily doesn't think I will be home this week more time in the hell hole of depression!

on a new drip & have to have it 5 x a day. Got one tonight at 10pm.

Emily said the things keeping me here are my mouth, liver, kidneys. And not peeing. Oh and diarrhoea.

Day + 27

30th August 2005.

Last night I had hardly any sleep couldn't get comfortable in bed, I felt breathless and kept going to the toilet. And had a drip till 12.30am then another 1 at 7am.

Was sick this morning it always happens in the norming with my first tablet.

My lips are going down with the new medication. The

doctors came to see me they say the same thing the reason im still in here is because of my kidneys & liver which is due to the medication ive had and they have taken me off the drip and put me on oral. Jessica may have Veno-occlussive Disease (VOD). Wrote by Emily I like Emily she always tells me the way it is. but the best way.

Me, mum and dad went to the cafe and met Lenny there He looked fit! Then we walked back to the hospital and sat outside for a while then came back to my room that when the doctor told me I have VOD! Bollocks! Another week longer in this place! Better to get it her than at home!

Laura came to visit me today on her week off! We had a good old chat & giggle met her boyfriend Paul.

Day + 28

31st August 05

Mum left at 8ish this morning and dad got here at 8ish aswel. Dad is staying with me all day. When mum left dad and I had a little snooze. Really breathless today, been on oxygen all day. Didn't have scan today to check for VOD, the thing keeping me in this horrible place. Got scan at 10am tomorrow.

My nan & Gramps came to visit today I want to go home with them!

Aunt Niki is staying tonight I miss my mum though!
Got Bone marrow at 4pm.
My lip is going down.

I should of stayed with you my lovely darling Jessie (mum) xxxx

1ˢᵗ September   ♥

Jessica had a hard nite last nite, she was coughing blood & hardly had no sleep, she has been out of her luxery apartment to a hostol with other patients, theres no shower or toilet to use or no privacy but its only for a couple of days until her plalets go up between 30-60. She has to use a oxygen mask because her lungs are week, I no she is strong enough to get through this last part because "my bitch is a fighter." Its 8.30 and the doctor said loraine might not be aloud to stay with her because its against the law! Jess is going to have a fit! Cant wait to I have got my beautiful best mate back at home with me, being her funny self, missed her so much! I hope she feels better tomorrow because she can only get stronger now.

Love you always Jessie Baby

xxx Daisy xxx

Can't believe Jes has had such a scary time over the last 2 days and I was not with her.

Nicky & Billy have been brilliant spliting themselves in half to be with jes & their daughter Claire who gave birth to a healthy 'Billy boy'! – Well nearly healthy he has a dodgy knee sounds like he make have a spot of 'Birditis' – you know when birds knees go backwards.

Billy gave me news when I was in Rome that Jes had taken a turn for the worst, I was fed up of those ruins anyway. Anita & I went to the 'Vatican – midnight on thurs 1st and again yesturday. We said enough prayers to shame the old bishops & wore our rosary beads out. We also managed to convert our friends. (now wouldn't our priests be proud of us!) Well the only reason I went to Rome was because 'Psychic Di' last May told me I would see my mum at 'the fountains' in Rome Well I went there and she did not contact me. Hours later I realised it was because she was looking after Jes. This morning Billy rang me and said to come back as Lorrane needed support.

I got the 11.30 flight from Rome to Gatwick. Ty picked me up. At last he has finished with Soraya – but for how long.

When I was with jes we held hands for 4 hrs. I cold not cry once I saw her cos I was so pleased to be with her & Lorrane.

The drugs arrived from Italy that she needed, the consultant is pleased that things have improved slowly. Her BP is going it nicely. Still has a high temp, is oedematas, jaundiced breathing still rapid & highly dependent on O^2. But, she will get over this high almost impossible wall & will abseil down.

Lorrane & I are staying night together. Each morning will bring brighter news & our beautiful Jes will shine through.

Sunday 4th September
Day 4 in H.D.U.
4th Sept 05

Jes had a good night. Lorraine & I stayed in the visitors room. Jes got the nurse to get either one of us on 3 occasions. Her temp is lower

1. Her ability to have O^2 through mask is tolerated 'off' for longer periods

2. Swelling in L) arm reduced

3.   Blood pressure lower & more stable

4.   Dr said liver & kidney results have improved

JESICA SAID she felt a bit better – Hooray! Jes still has fluid in the lungs so was given more d.wenos – within 1 hr. BP reduced further & urine output improved.

Jes wrote to Dr 'is the risk of me dieing smaller?' He was a bit gutted but said 'yes defnately smaller as there have been improvements but obviously things could go wrong but as she is constantly being assessed her chances are better. Jes wrote that she felt more positive 'aunty deby is really helping me. I love her sooo much' 'as usual mum is here but I could not be without her.

The nurse here are very kind and competent Jes feels safe in this knowledge. Jes loves Billy & Nic for being there for her. Billy told Jes yesturday he would get her a Range Rover! Jes wants the four of us to go to a health farm. Cant wait

4/9/05

Me and Romina came to see JESSICA today. I was really nervous cos I hadn't seen her in so long. I shed a tear! I know she is getting better. I bought her present all the way from LA. The JESSICA number plate will look well good in your mini cooper!! You can drive us around. I pray I past my test on Monday. Me and you are gonna go for a spin if I pass. I'll probably get too nervous just like in school!

I gave the best massage on her trotters. You have the funniest toe. I think my massage was so good, she fell asleep. The red top will look brill on you.

This was my first visit and I wish I'd been up more. I told you about Laurens row. She nearly hit the girl but some boy was holding her back. I have never seen her get that mad in my whole life.

You best be better for my 18th

Love your bestestbumchums

Leah Romina

4/9/05

Hello be jefro

How u doing its realy nice to see you. Hope leah passes her test she can take us all for a spin.

Luv ya mills and trills

Romina

Xxx

4th September 2005

Jess seems so much brighter today than yesterday, she has had a scarey couple of days, but she is improving slowly which is very good imformation for her, hopefully this will continue, I can tell she is getting better & better, we just have to stay positive coz she will get through this because she is a true fighter. I am writing this with Romina & lea massageing her feet. She loves to be treated like a little princesses. Lenny & jeff have been up which is good. Lorain & Debbie have gone to meet Phil. They both had a really ruff night last night because they both slept on chairs pushed together in the visitors room, brought some pancakes up for them this morning. Cant wait for to come home

Love you always

Stay strong!

Daisy

Xxxxx

Jess, just a quicky. You are looking great!! Cant believe how well you are doing. Don't forget there are ups and there are downs. You will have both but soon enough you will be higher than ever. Fully recovered!

Anyway, take care, love you.

Tyrone

Jessica WHITMORE
6th SEPTEMBER 2005
12.10 R.I.P.

Note by the publisher, James Essinger:

The following comments by friends and family were written in Jessie's diary after her passing. The writers were all in shock and very distressed and often wrote in a rather stream of consciousness way without much regard to spelling. I've decided to keep the spelling and phrasing verbatim as it was to show the emotional authenticity of the moment.

09-07-06

Jessie has been dead for 10 months – I miss her so much since Jessie's death Geoff and I don't live togeather anymore I have a flat in Larkfield, he is in the process of buy a place in Sidcup Ryan is renting a place with 2 of his mates Jessie's school St Catherine;s have had a memorial and planted a tree in her memory. St Lukes College that she attended have had a memorial and on 13/7/06 there is going to be a remembrance ceremony – On the 30th June 06 was Jessie's 18th Birthday. I invited some of her friends, my family attended Jessie's boyfriend Lenny I had 18 red helium red balloons and we all wrote messages on the balloons and let them all fly away of my balcony after they all flew away that lovely butterfly flew by right by Lennie & Ryan.

Life at the moment is very sad for me. I miss her so much I find some of her clothes that she has never worn. Notes that she used to write to me when I was looking for something once I found a piece of paper in the coffee table and it said

"I wear white. I wear wings, my hair in curls and I do good things. I didn't want to leave I didn't want to go I left you with no good bye and now your all alone." (There was a small arrow at the top of the page pointing up.)

Aunty Deby – written 9th May 2006.

Jessi's last few days were the most, incredulous, sad, & up-lifting at times of courage and strength. The following is what I remember, as if yesturday, and how I felt at the time.

4th September 2006

Ironically the last entry at the time was from Tyrone stating how 'well' jes looked. This was the 4th September She was in High Dependancy unit (had been for 4 days). On that Sunday things took a turn for the better. Two days before she was told she had less than a 10% chance of surviving if she had to be put on a ventilator. She was awaiting some pioneering drugs from Italy which may help to reverse her condition. (She had 'bleeding' in her lungs) The drugs had arrived on the 3rd – 1 hour after I had returned from Rome she seemed brighter today and wrote on a piece of paper 'I feel more positive today'. Certain observations were improving. The Consultant Anaethetist came round and said if she continues to improve she would be off her 'sealed' oxygen mask by Tuesday. Jes had lots of her friends vising her. Lorrane & I went for a few drinks. Strange we were elated and happy for a change. Lorrane & Geoff have been so sad not knowing the outcome. How they must have felt and coped with Jessica's deterioration and not only their knowledge but Jessica also, knowing, her condition seemed hopeless (all but 10%). That mere 10% chance seems hopeless until you are told 5% then suddenly any chance is good. Only they will know Jessi lay in her bed, determined to keep that very uncomfortable mask on. Hourly Jes tried drinking. She even had Weetabix in the morning. When the mask would have to come off. She would be struggling to breathe, her lips would go blue. The mask was so light it was cutting into her face which was swelling anyway.

She let everyone tickle her legs. Lorrane went home that eve in the knowledge that just maybe the light was coming through & God was sparing Jes.

Ryan visited – jes loved him visiting and caring for her so much. Ty came, Jess with all her discomfort tried to give the ward sister his mobile number as he fancied her. True to form Jes in her last hours thought of others and was brave & positive.

That eve we watched 'X factor' she felt better and said she was wanted to go home. I said to Jessica that the Psychic had told me if I went to Rome I would see my mum. I told jes that I didn't see her cause all the time she was looking after her.

5th September 06

Jes only needed me twice in the night. I was sleeping on a mattress in visitors room. at 05.45 I came to her. she was more breathless when I tried to clean her mouth.

In the morning round there was talk of jes having to go to Intensive Care This was most alarming as jes knew that if there she had less chace of survival. Could see jessi's worried fact Rang Billy & Lorrane to come to ward.

Dr's came to jes while lorry & I were with her. Jes wanted me to ask Doctor what her chances were if she went to I.T.U. He said 'the chances are 5% of surviving but that he doubted if she would get off the ventilator. I tried to cheer things up by saying she was positive & young & that most people in ITU are old so more chance of dieing.

That afternoon jes went to ITU lorry Geof, Ryan, Tyrone, Billy, Nic, lucy, laura B (they were tearing themselves in half cos cousin clare had just had a billy baby Daisy – her best friend, Lenny her beloved boyfriend, Caroline, Glen, alan, tanya, sarah lennys mum & sister. All visited jes Jes was in her room. Her eyes darting from one person to another. She indicated she had back pain. A few hours later Father Doyle – her catholic priest visited. He did not wanted to frighten her with 'the last rights' – he was great. Jessi put her hand out to him and wanted to say prayers with him. They prayed together. Lorrane said she seemed suddenly more at ease.

It was true. 9pm onwards that evening jess was cool. The nurse looking after her said that her Carbon dioxide levels were too high, if they got to a certain level she would have to go on the ventilator. We were dreading that moment.

We took turns to go in, at one point lenny's mum kissed her & cried jes wrote on a piece of paper & gave to lorrane 'len mum cried'

6th September 2006

Well into the night & morning we prayed talked, laughed. Near 04.00 The ward charge nurse said she would have to go on the ventilator.

The anaethetist came. Geof, Ryan, Lorraine & I stood round the bed, as the bed end went down jes motioned to her eyes – I – then her heart – Love – her finger went round the bed and pointed to us all – You all – I tried to cheerfully say, let your lungs rest jes and we will see you in a few days.

Lorry said 'I don't want you to go jes' The anaesthetist said 'OK jessi we will see you soon'

We left. While jes was prepared we were told she would be on the ventilator for 5-6 days. My worry then was only, if she does not improve would they persue with a tracheostomy. We came back at 05.00. Geof went home or to work. Billy, lorry & I wondered the hospital and strangely were joking around. They told us jes still had not been fully prepared & to go home

Lorry & I were take by Billy to Jack's we slept for 2-3 hours. At 10.00 I rang the unit & asked if we could bring a c.d. player for music.

Jes was going to be turned on her front at 11.00 hrs to see if the fluid would loosen.

lorrane & I went to nic & billys, to get the c.d player. We stupidly decided to go to see Claire & the new baby.
If only, if only we hadn't.

***

after an hour we made our way to Kings hospital. Only got as far as longfield and we got a call from Geof to say that jes had deteriorated & to get their a.s.a.p. I speeded & hoped to get pulled over by the police so we could get a police escort.

No – it never happens when you want it.

We were frantic, lorry rang the unit they said they would keep jess 'alive' till we got their. we did quite good timing 30 mins, 13.20 lorry went up to the unit. I parked the car.

When I got to the ward, I went into jes's room. She was breathless, still, pale Geof, lorry, Ryan, the priest & a stranger was there. The unseen stranger of a priest was giving the last rights, the unknown stranger was supporting lorrane. Geof's mum & Dad were there.

Unbelievable, inconceivable – our jes had gone. Lorrane had not even been there when she died. apparently she had been turned over, she then had to be resuscitated. Her death was 12.10. Geof & ryan were there at 11.50 so was Geof's Mum & dad. Thank god people she loved were with her.

R.I.P. our dearest bravest
    Shining Jes.